THE ZEN OF KEN

Kenneth F. Conklin

Copyright© 2021 Kenneth F. Conklin
ISBN: 978-81-8253-748-4

First Edition: 2021
Rs. 200/-

Cyberwit.net
HIG 45 Kaushambi Kunj, Kalindipuram
Allahabad - 211011 (U.P.) India
http://www.cyberwit.net
Tel: +(91) 9415091004
E-mail: info@cyberwit.net

Printed at in India at VCORE CONNECT LLP.

INTRODUCTION

The poems presented in this book were composed beginning in the late 1960's and continue to the present. They reflect my emotional reaction and resulting mood set by the circumstances encountered at the time. I never intended to be a poet. I simply use the words to set a cathartic path for the closing or opening of whatever door my life's journey has encountered.

Music was and continues to be a source of inspiration for my poetry. As the words flow from pen to paper (or fingers to keyboard) a tune is often running through my head. I discovered early on that I am moved by songs with lyrics with a strong emotionally impact. Initially it was the words of songwriters such as Jackson Browne, Bob Dylan, Carol King, Bernie Taupin, and Joni Mitchell. I often transposed the lyrics of these great poets - as that is what they truly are - to paper while listening to the music containing them. Later, I was taken by the words of Mississippi bluesmen Willie Dixon, Robert Johnson, and Chester Burnett and many others. After absorbing the words I imagined what events motivated their creation.

For example, Bob Dylan's dystopian song *All Along the Watchtower* with the climatic lines "Two riders were approaching and the wind began to howl" was his emotional reaction to a business negotiation involving rights to his work. Reading lyrics such as "businessmen, they drink my wine . . ." without the distraction of the instrumental music made the metaphorical connection for me.

The poems here are not presented in chronological order. They are grouped more or less by mood. I admit the ones collected in The Dark Ages section are mostly earlier ones and the ones in The Age of Enlightenment section are more recent as that is how my life has progressed. The pieces that make up the Haiku Interludes follow the 5-7-5 syllabic tradition but their tone is in the modern style rather than the traditional Japanese form.

I hope you take your time with these personal reflections. I look forward to hearing from you about their resonance with your own life's journey.

Contents

THE DARK AGES

A World Without

What happens to the sound,
When all that is left is silence?
And the leaves are dormant on their branches
While the wind has lost its violence.

What happens to the blood
Without a heart beat to propel it?
Soldier's weapons are on the ground
Their cause has been negated.

Mr. Blue Bird is on my shoulder
It has no where else to go;
It is frightened for the future
Its song has lost its soul.

Horrific is the scene before us
Smoldering remnants do remain;
The battle lost by someone
The others are left insane.

What happens to the sound
When the clock has stopped its motion?
And the blood puddles in muddy ground
In a world without emotion.

Agent Orange!

The Chinook bore down on us
While waiting to go on to the next clearing
Carved from the jungle
By an alien force
A place we could defend the intangible.

Incoming said the Doppler
I knew the difference between the sound
Of in and out
Explosions, chaos!
The Chinook flew away.

I inhaled the dust and it found me
Making its way through my cells
Attacking me in latent ways
Lying in wait for the right time
To attack.

While Captain Boyd who found his end earlier
Is on the Wall
I saw him there when I visited, to say hi
And tell him the Chinook did return and take me away
But the remnants remain, to this day . . .

The Metastasized Waltz

It all started
A long time ago
Rooted in key places
Where I would not be found
Until I could not
Hide any more

I grew up you see
And like a child leaving home
I left the confines
Of my sanctuary to see
What else was out there
And to express myself

Once I got going
It was easy to move around
Welcomed here and welcomed there
The space time continuum
Not an impedance
To coming of my gospel

I am everywhere now
In key locations
Spreading the nature
Of my existence
But there is a rebellion now
Slowing my progress

I am tired
Of laying down my tracks
I might just settle down right here
Where I can hide out
Or lay low
Until the quiet comes, again.

Darling of Darkness

Darling of darkness
Where are you now
I've danced on dark clouds
I've played on the bow
I've tried new roads
And looked at the old
Marched up and down alleys
Stood out in the cold
Lived by the clock
With no sense of time
Spent a lot on nothing
With my last dime
Told people about me
Without listening to them
Fallen deeply in love
And back out again
Fallen deeper still
Didn't like the trash
Learned not to kill
But paid in cash
Been up to the top
To see what was there
Saw nothing I wanted
But stood there to stare
Now I am floating
In space without air
Hoping to find
Someone to share

All the dreams of my mind
And thoughts of despair
But mostly I need
Someone who cares

Liberty Bell

Watching waiting where we please
Peaceful pleasant pleading trees
Touching trunks talk to me
Maybe they will let me be

Whistling warriors will wage war
Finagling financiers fall for more
Troubled times take from me
All I want is to be free

The Old Man

The old man walks
  down cobweb streets
Listening for
  some distant beat
When all was right
  long ago
When he was young
  long ago
He walks on and on
  through graying stone
On broken walks
  and old dead bones
Such a long time
  since he cried
Such a long time
  Since he tried

And as he walks he wonders why
He hasn't found his piece of sky

The Orphan

A hungry child
Came to me and said:
"Please take me in
My mommy's dead
My daddy's gone
Far away
From me who needed
Him to stay
Please take me in
And hold me tight
Hide me from sin
And awful fright
and the sound of guns
and the hell of war
I'm just a child
Don't close the door

Post Trauma

A jungles fury has gone by
To dead men lying in ships that fly
People dying in unborn minds
People crying, lost in time
Gone is lost in the distant past
It really cost but it did not last
Needed to feel, needed to unfold
For those who want stories untold
War is gone, so is cause
So are the people in the mirage
It was long ago, it was far away
And it all came back when I cried today

The Darkening

The trees are blowing loudly now
Gemini has gone away
The world is oblivious now
Children forgot to play

Scenes of love have vanished now
Politicians hung up their cause
Houses have become monuments now
Doctors without their gauze

Kissing is obsolete now
Bars are full of beer
Peace is just a word now
No one sheds a tear

I am sitting crying now
My cause is not too clear
The lull before the storm now
Don't know who to fear

Ghetto People

Dancing in the dark
In and out of life
Listening to the dog bark
The lonely human strife
Pleasing only oneself
Needing only them
Standing on the empty shelf
A glass bottle gem
Ghetto people standing around
The closing open door
Living in the lost and found
Fighting the hot war
Love passing us all by
Standing in the dark
Throwing in the last pie
Naked in the park
Love of life is in the clear
No curtain strings attached
Dirty old men drinking beer
Shirts have all been patched
A cold wind has started blowing
Coming from the west
The lovers have all parted knowing
None ever gave their best

Once

Thinking about what I once had
Thinking about why it went bad
Or maybe it really was for
Opening up another door
Giving me a peak
Of I'm here again

Danger, lurking

TV blaring
In the dark of noon
People caring
In the midnight doom
Heightened perils
Do not cease
For Egyptian pharaohs
And Northern geese
The garbage man
In the bright of dawn
Admires his tan
On the desert lawn
Danger lurks
Around the bend
From adamant Turks
And the southern friend
Camps are full
Of flimsy tents
In the solid mall
Of accidents

Persevering

Listen to the mockingbirds
Listen to them call
They're asking what gives here
Why can't you stand tall

Why do I always have to be
The one that's always strong
Can't anybody ever see
That I can't stand it very long

Either always be happy and gay
Or don't be here at all
And don't you ever ever say
I am about to fall

Give me love, let me feel
Give me a chance at life
And if I falter and start to fall
Just light another light

The Hollow Hours

In the early morning mist
Of yesterday's doom
We saw them running far away
We saw them run too soon

In tomorrow's evening pride
The place we call the twilight time
We saw them running far away
We saw them not stop in time

Dancing in the hollow hours
Waltzing in the dark
Walking up to the next in line
Let me listen to your bark

The lions roar is now silent
The demon's curse subdued
I don't know what gets me here
Its like standing in the nude

Ten thousand people asking what
Ten thousand more, why?
Some ways are just really safe
Others don't ever try

Epilogue

Please don't remember me by
  what I wrote today
I want you to remember
  the way we used to play

I'm angry and I'm bitter now
  over doing something wrong
But please don't take it out on me
  I'm not always the one that's strong

HAIKU INTERLUDE

Dodger Stadium

the seagull landed
the spectators oohed and awed
strike one cried the ump

Eons

mars saturn venus
moon lurking between each one
blink an eye its gone

Simpler Times

california sun
running down the one oh one
melancholy time

First Snow

the sheer silence stirs
footprints cross the whiteness
a dog barks harshly

An Author's Lament

i wrote those words now
and wonder who will read them
here's wishing they will

Wintering in Greenfield

walking greenfield trails
the lake ripples when birds land
joggers impact mud

A Winter Deluge

rain is falling now
the robins are sheltering
while big rigs brake hard

Talking Heads

the noise is nonstop
with animated gestures
the sun lights the east

THE MIDDLE AGES

Not Being

I really feel
that if I could
approach it with zeal
then I know I would
find a place
just to be
without space
or have to see
the march of time
the absence of free
the subtle line
of going to be.

Leaving Fourth Street

I will leave behind my gardening tools
And the special shelves
I built for the kitchen pantry
The ocean continues to pound
As it always has while
The seagulls circle and screech
I will never open this front door again
To my home at the beach

The bamboo branches are mourning
While the moving van is loaded
With all my stuff, eastward bound
Its diesel engine idling
I wave good bye to neighbors
(Come see us soon)
I will never open this front door again
To my home at the beach

While my favorite chair is finally loaded
As is the 'To Beach' sign pointing west
Be well old eucalyptus friend
Be at one with the salt laced breeze
Why won't someone convince me to stay!
Or reinstate the job I lost
I will never leave for just the day again
And return to my home at the beach

They Don't Make Forever Like They Used To

At the One Half Lounge
Crooning 'Sail Away'
Or, 'Georgia on My Mind'
Or, 'Pour Me Another Vacation'

Sometimes meeting me at Muddy Waters
Drinking coffee, lamenting about the times
Paranoia setting in
Pettiness robbing your genius

You finally let go of the drugs
And the alcohol
Never the women, though
And certainly never the artistry

And such songs they were
With Hendrix and Webb
With some Sinatra sprinkled in
To keep us grounded

And at the Iridium
When Les Paul himself invited you on stage
You brought the house down
As you knew you would

In the key of 'Wichita Lineman'
You painted a picture, for me
An oriental 'Irisis"
And to this day it is there

And the time you cried
Letting your Bukowski
shield down
Your uncloaked heart showing
Your brilliance, misunderstood

You would hate
That YouTube has you now
But you welcomed the band of angels
Saying, Sheldon

We are coming to carry you home
We are coming to carry you home

The Cocoon

Aching bones and muggy air
Permeate my psyche
But it's cool inside
My cocoon
Waiting for the next thing
To come along
And grab me
And pull me to the next level
Where bigger things
Will occupy my conscious

Seeking

The light is there, somewhere
I am searching for it, with some direction
But more so with the back of my hand
Carefully touch each wall, looking for the crack
The door knob, something unlocked
Something to emerge into where I will get traction again,
Like I once achieved just briefly and felt all cylinders firing
In the meantime, no panic, just heading for the light
Wherever it is

Just like Hunter

Getting my kicks on Hollywood Blvd
In Barre, Vermont
Where Jackson Browne played
For his friend, Warren
And me, I am writing about it
Folding it into Gallery House
Connecting the dots
From LA to Barre to Roanoke
Thinking about my obituary
Which I think I better write
As that is what I have will become
One more dead writer
To be remembered
Like Warren Zevon and Hunter Thompson
Or just one more person on Hollywood Blvd

Rest Stop, Closed

There must be one coming up soon
I keep looking
Watching for that special place
When I can breathe (and smile) for real
When the breaths are deep
And pleasure is sleep
For twenty minutes or so
Ah, but it is closed
Time to keep moving on
Just turn it off, I keep saying
I do not need to answer that
And what would happen to my world
If the rest came, finally
Would it stop, would they care?
Not me, so just do it!

Basement Blues

In my basement, alone
The world goes on above me
A shower, doors opening, footsteps
Loudly pounding life beats
Coming up for air sometimes
Smiles look my way at my arrival
Resuming conversations, about the weather
About the kids today
Won't live up to the greatest generation
Oh, but they will
They are not underground
No basement for them
Where I am
Keeping busy, very busy with my stuff

What is it Good For?

I now understand what is meant
By the words "the art of war"
Oh, the power that comes with
Ordering men and women into battle
Knowing their heads will be lopped
Off at the neck and their limbs will fly
And the blood will flow
The art of it, the power of it
You are god, at your command
They will charge un-abandoned for you
Screaming and yelling, such a primal urge
This existence
This precious life that will end
At the end of a sword or in a bed, alone.

Main Street Sweeper

Dressed in white
Broom in hand
The people pass
Hand in hand

Troubles are gone
Glitter then
In Fantasyland
Everywhere and there

But what about
The underground
Where all is
Lost and found

And where do
The mothers go
When their lives
Become inconsequential

The main street sweeper
Goes on and on
From the depot tracks
To the castle's throng.

Ode For the Young

Oh tender youth
please don't lose
the qualities
that make you young

Oh tender youth
please always be
the one
we rely upon

Oh tender youth
please show no patience
with out
concrete ways

Oh tender youth
do not take for granted
for like us
you will pay.

Nostalgia

Soothing hearts
are made to play
among the mystic eyes

Heavy loads
are hard to bear
amidst the lovers sighs

Happy days
are far removed
and lost among the trees

Old men
long for the war
and children on their knees.

A Broad Brush

Painting the sky
   full of browns
   and blacks and blues
   with a patch of red
   filling the earth
   dancing with shadows
   of yesterday's dreams
   and positioning
   tomorrow's schemes
   and planning and worry
   about the troubles
   today will bring when
   the L. A. Times
   comes waltzing in
   on mornings of green
   and summers of rain
   the clouds above
   still bring tales of woe
   and trees in parks
   full of dirt and mud

And in my head
All of the above

Things that Feel

I'm surrounded by silent stills
of window sills
and lonely ghosts
and unpaid bills
and wait until's
but are they real
these things that don't feel

People passing every day
in castle cars
they seemingly say
"see what I have and what you got
see what I do and see what I bought
and see what I've learned
what I've been taught
and you better not squeal
cause I've never been caught"
but are they real
these things that don't feel

The President called
on his hotline phone
he said "Ken, my man,
adjust your tone
I need the people to follow me
I need you on an even keel
to make them see
that the way I feel
will make them be

stamped with my seal
of things that don't feel"

I awoke this morning
it was a sunny day
the birds were singing
the children at play

the laughter I heard was very real
I thought how nice it is to feel
and I solemnly promised
from this day on
that never again
will I be stepped upon
by those who pretend not to deal
with the important things
the things that feel!

Underground

In the misty sunlight
Stands a man who found his trade
Selling roses
Beneath the moon in the city
Where the people lie
Underground
When the tired businessman
Came looking around
For the woman who needed him
When he was just a young man
Fighting Sam
Oh please try it next time
But don't stand in the sunlight
As the moon goes down
Underground
In the city where the roses grow

Searching for My Baby

I've been searching for my baby
In the middle of the woods
I've been searching for my baby
And her bill of goods

I've been marching up the highway
Looking for some shoulds
Been searching for my baby
In the middle of the woods

Found her standing in the clearing
Hoping she would see
Her hair was flying wildly
It was unencumbered you see

I saw her standing in the clearing
Wanting to be free
But I caught up to her in the clearing
And she decided not to flee

Puerto Vallarta

When the sea has cast its soft spray
upon the rock lined shore
and the throng has completed the ritual
from Aztecs and España plays out
amongst the shadows displayed for el sol
as breezes linger amongst the palms
and where the sea pounds
the remaining resistance through the town
we turn and note the irrelevancy
of our call

Waiting for Santa

Where does this coldness come from
when once there was sensitivity
and my body cried of emotion
but now when told of terrible things
like I just was abut my mother's cancer
probably spreading again
how my reaction is not of alarm or panic
but of a calm aloofness that is numbing and
i wonder if she knows how distant I have become
since she became inert and non functioning
as an intellectual anymore
someone I can no longer talk to
or converse with and
with whom I can only share pleasantries and weather,
not like when I was young
just home from high school or
when we talked
while I was in the large skyscraper in Atlanta
or that magic night at the marina
sipping drinks at the formica bar
in front of the mock fire place
when we were waiting for Santa Claus

Dale

Oh little one
Oh little one
I love to see you run

Oh little one
Oh little one
Your blonde hair in the sun

Big blue eyes
Dance with wonder
At every sound of laughter
Or sudden clap of thunder

Oh little one
Oh little one
Your life has just begun

HAIKU INTERLUDE,
CONTINUED

Jazz Talking

snarky puppy chords
sparking synapsed ideas
origins abound

An Author's Delight

a well-known author
just said he will be reading
the book I wrote – yay

The Swamp

it has more odor
I thought it was to be drained
instead its toxic

Christmas Eve

waiting for santa
with Mom at the marina
see the comets streak!

The Day After

twas the day after
snow turned to ice on the ground
presents all unwrapped

Like a Waterfall

words flow like water
placid and rapid at times
then over the dam

A Writer's Lament

punctuation time
semi colon or comma
oops delete delete

2021

a doe stands very still
twenty twenty one is here
the mist is clearing

The Week That Was

the birds sing their songs
and gather sticks for their nests
the circus leaves town

THE AGE OF
ENLIGHTENMENT

Breaking Rock

They sent me here, to learn
About what my life is
Its purpose I found
As I pound, the Rock
In the distance I see Johannesburg
The people cry out my name
I am here for you I say
But do they hear, do they hear while I am
Breaking Rock
There is no hate, there is no get even
This is for you, to be free
I will not give in, ever so I will maintain while
Breaking Rock
They cry out now: Nelson!
Lead us, and I will
The world knows me now
Important people, but I am just a man
Breaking Rock
So you will break the Bonds, and you will be free
There is no hate, there is no level field
Just now, breaking Rock, with an eye on the future
I am Mandela!

Knight of Love

I don't ride any white horse
I don't own a set of armor
Men don't shake when I come around
I'm certainly not a charmer

My castle is made only of flesh
I can't shield my feelings
Kings and Queens don't fill me in
On all their social dealings

My moat went dry years ago
While fighting the dragon's flame
I successfully saved my kingdom
But the sword won the game

I finally laid my armor down
Ran naked through the desert
I stumbled on you at an oasis
Trying to wash away the dirt

Now naked, I can't save you
I'm no god from above
But all I've ever really wanted
Is just to share my love

The Empty Saddle

Dancing on a moonlight beam
The children laughed an played
We do not know from where they came
Or why they didn't stay

Their laughter filled us all with joy
Their songs are full of life
Its wonderful to hear them sing
While we clean our knives

The part of us that's speaking now
Used to be standing idle
But it came out while missing the one
Belonging to the empty saddle

Someday we will ride the moon
Via the sun's luminous rays
And we can thank the riderless horse
For showing us the way

The Treasure

After so many years
 of mining the cold grey hills
Picking and digging with tears
 finding only those who kill
My pick and my shovel
 turning dirt and stirring dust
Hacking away at granite
 no gold, only another bust
Hiking mile upon mile
 hoping thru the passage of time
I would find my just reward
 but I found only grime

One day while roaming the desert
(after giving up my mountain hunt)
I found a rose blooming brightly in the sun
And I took you by the hand
And walked into the bright sunlight
Never to return to the shaft
But always to eternally cherish
The precious treasure of you

The Walk

Walking in the wild
　　Early in the morning
I met a beautiful girl
　　Who walked a while with me
She talked about a lover
　　Who was untrue to her
I told her about my lover
　　Who took me for a fool

We walked a little further
　　In the early morning rain
We walked a little longer
　　In our early morning pain

Walking in the wild
　　Early in the morning
I met a beautiful girl
　　Who shared it all with me

Ruby

My birthstone is the Ruby
Bright, solid, and clear
Never knew what it meant before
All I knew was fear

My feelings have all been felt before
But never quite this way
The words don't come too easy
Don't really know what to say

Talking to you soft and easy
Watching you really care
Did not really know
It was so really easy to share

Vibes of Fate

It was unexpected
The way you came into my life
Like a welcome breeze
Just like I had always known you
To remind me to
Enjoy the sunshine
And the fate
Of whatever happens
Is supposed to happen
For us to learn from
As I have learned from you
Transposing your energy
And quiet vibes
To everything I do
And to make me
Recognize with each passing year
The astounding presence
Of you in my life

An Awakening

Looking out on the twilight sky
There is no doubt I really can fly
Saw a vision but it was real
Love walked in and made me feel
That it is alright I'm no longer alone
In the endless night its really known
I can touch it, feeling young
My candle has been lit
No more hunger
Feeling no pain
Can throw away
My crutch and cane
Won't hold back any more
No reason to close the door
Or shut the window from the sun
Cause I just met
Not just anyone
But honest beauty
And sweet brown eyes
And the loving sound
Of midnight sighs

Time

When the tide has turned my dear
When the tide has turned
When the sun sets onto steaming water
And the moon shines continuously upon the night
Then there will be the passage into
The next generations of winters thaw
And time travels on from where we go
Through eternal tunnels and infinite space
And deep within souls of unending life
Our existence flows from photonic sparks
Of glitter and stone and lives on as one

My Valentine

Deeply in love
Am I with you
From the beginning
To the now and new
Made from ordinary days
Not knowing, but
Letting it take us
On to the next one
And grateful that
It is you with me
Hand in hand
Forever, deeply in love

A Christmas Poem to Barbara

Christmas in Daleville
Cozy inside, alone with you
The mist gathers outside, wet and cool
While we read our books and talk
And cheerfully toast the upcoming year
Looking forward to what it will bring
Here and afar, but cozy inside together
Alone with you.

Another Christmas Poem to Barbara

The sun is rising over the hill
It's Christmas morning in Daleville
Clouds are gleaming against an orange lattice
The golf course is an empty green canvas
A quiet time for you and me
A Christmas morning in Daleville
Our tree is still standing, a miracle I'd say
But then again it is Christmas day

Mother's Day, 2016

In the spring
When nests are built
The children gather
To be with you
They are grateful
For all they have
And they have learned
From being with you
And when they are down
Who do they call?
Who do they reach?
Always, it is you
And you tell them
As mothers do
Things will be fine
And they are with you

Christmas, 2016

Another Christmas in Daleville with family and you
Happy times abound, with music too
A time to be grateful for all that we have
And time to look back on our well-travelled path

To another year with you, with music and new roads
And absorbing our lives with all that it bodes
Merry Christmas to us and to all who we love
Family and friends and to all that we tend

A Mother's Day

They who did not know you
Two boys, three girls
Wanting to grow, to make a life
Each one fighting to make it
Somewhere, somehow
All wanting and wanting
Like birds, beaks turned upward
And there you were
For each one
Feeding and nurturing
Individually, for each is different
And now, all grown up
Have made their own nests
Yet still they call
To you and pass on
All you have shown
About living, about enjoying
About appreciation
You are theirs, forever

At Muddy Waters

At Muddy Waters
Burlington, Vermont
Bernie the senator just came and went
Ordering a French Roast
Elvis Presley playing over the sound system
Then some Lucinda Williams
Here comes the tourette person
Grunting and groaning
The possibly female UVM student
With their possibly female mentor
Discussing Karl Marx
But short skirts are now in here
A street person just came in
Or maybe he's a college professor
Wishing he was something different
The old man keeps writing in his usual perch
While people and cars move down Main Street
And now comes Radio Head over the sound system
At Muddy Waters
Burlington, Vermont

Celebration Time

In the early evening hours
And the sun is setting down
The birds look our way
To see if we're around
They know that we know
This is their time of day
They are splashing in the pond
And communing in the maze
While we take it all in
Reading, talking as we do
Celebration time it is
For the past, present, and new
During those early evening hours

My Sign

Its growing now
I know it is
Can't see it, can't feel it
Except in my heart
Which is breaking
I like living and watching
The sun rising, the sun setting
Each day
While the North Star at night
With accompanying wind chill
Which is picking up now
Where now is that cancer sign
Can't see it in the sky
Can't feel it in my body
It is there
I know it is.
Driving me from this world
Someday
Leaving me in the breeze
Brushing against everyone I knew
When I was in the daylight

Shy Anger Review

a perfect escape for election night
when an escape is calling
talking heads telling me
what I already know
insulting my intelligence
when Shy Anger lets me escape
massaged my real feelings
and let me breathe
freely

Visiting with Evy

What those eyes have seen
Wizened, alert
Days on the farm
Then in town
Cars, tractors, and cows
Husband, son, work days
All gone
Worried about forgetting
And Oprah
Please keep these photos
Keep moving, stay steady
My Daddy was important
Where is the respect?
But, who remembers
Except me
And this faded photo of him and mom
Oh, what those eyes have seen
In one hundred years

Nieu Amsterdam Sunrise

First light appeared
As a faint glow
On the horizon
Where sea meets sky
Brighter it grew
The crowd gathered
Welcoming quietly
And thinking I am here
For one more turn
Of the planet
Conscious for another day
Learning for another day
Appreciating for another day
The birth of someone
The death of someone
And the daily exposure
Of infinite creation

The Open Road

Trooper, trooper
hear my plea
I've come in here
to set you free

This road you travel
is all you see
There's more out there
so come with me

This land we're in
goes up and down
Not like this highway
with no sound

Around every turn
is a mystery
But to leave this road
you must be free

Another Christmas Song

Just another Christmas song
Just another prayer
Just another word of joy
Just to show we care

Just another thank you note
To show we know right from wrong
Just another servant
Trying to sing your song

You were born to die for us
You were born to care
You left us with the word of God
And taught us the holy prayer

Christmas is such a sacred time
But we have done it wrong
We need to remember you by it
And sing of it in song

Just another thank you note
To show we know right from wrong
Just another servant
Trying to sing your song

Just another word of joy
Just show we care
Just another Christmas song
Just another prayer.

A Saturday Afternoon

Saturday afternoon again
And I'm lying in bed with you
Its not just every now and then
Its always when skies are blue

Its really nice to see your face
Its good to be here with you
Ever since you started coming around
Its hard ever to be blue

Sometimes in the still of night
And sometimes in the bright of day
And sometimes not at just any time
You come to me and we play

Hope I always can feel this way
Hope its always there
Because when you come to play
I know you really care

The Zen of Ken

A Tuesday morning and feeling good
About all that is ahead and how we got here
From California to Virginia, from Paris to New Zealand
An adventure like no other
And times that live forever
When long ago when I was young
I wrote of the future about life at the top
About seeing nothing I wanted
But stood there to stare
Well I am staring and consuming
But moving away now, moving away
To a place of zen, the place of ken

Made in the USA
Columbia, SC
14 July 2021